SCHIRMER'S LIBRARY
OF MUSICAL CLASSICS

JEAN BAPTISTE CRAMER

Fifty
Selected Piano-Studies

Systematically Arranged, Fingering and
Expression-Marks Critically Revised,
and Provided with Instructive Notes by
DR. HANS VON BÜLOW

Translations by
ALBERT R. PARSONS and B. BOEKELMAN

Newly Revised by
DR. THEODORE BAKER

(Complete) — Library Vol. 827

G. SCHIRMER, Inc.

DISTRIBUTED BY

7777 W. BLUEMOUND RD. P.O. BOX 13819 MILWAUKEE, WI 53213

PREFACE.

To mention in detail, and with a mere repetition of encomiums, what is universally recognized and has often been said concerning the inestimable value and enduring importance of J. B. Cramer's pianoforte-studies, as a cultural means for the pianist's execution and delivery, (a means not only unexcelled, but also—with the exception of Muzio Clementi's "Gradus ad Parnassum", for which they serve as the most suitable preparation—one as yet but approximately equalled by any other collection of studies,) can not, of course, be the purpose of these lines. If Fétis, the Romanic musical authority of the present, designates them as "éminemment classiques", and if, of his German colleagues, Franz Brendel and C. F. Weitzmann, the former, in his history of music, terms them "a foundation marking a new epoch for all solid study"; and the latter, in his history of pianoforte-playing.* [Engl. translation, New York, 1893], numbers them among the classics of pianoforte-literature in respect alike to contents and form, these consonant opinions of the most renowned æstheticians and theorists really but state a fact, the great consequence of which speaks to us most loudly in the universal dissemination and popularity of the work here newly issued to the public in a specifically *instructive* edition. Perhaps it will not be superfluous to say a few words in justification of the new edition (or elaboration), although only through careful inspection of the work itself will the purpose of the editor become perfectly clear. The need of such an instructive edition has been often felt already. Louis Berger (born 1777. and Clementi's pupil from 1804-10) deemed it necessary to edit the first twelve studies with additional directions for the fingering; the entire work was afterward similarly edited by Julius Knorr ; while, quite recently, Mr. Louis Köhler has issued, as the opening book of his "Classical High School for Pianists", a selection of thirty studies, with glosses in part highly useful. It is idle critically to review the editions named, since the new one here submitted originated solely in their criticism. The old need has simply remained unsatisfied. and the attentive observer of the doings of the pianoforte-playing world can not escape the perception of how seldom it is—in proportion to their universal dissemination—that the cultural material proffered in Cramer's studies is exhaustively utilized; while their well-considered and methodic employment must have for its result the gain of a firm foundation for virtuoso-discipline in the good sense, nay, the gain of an already comparatively developed degree of mechanical and intellectual ripeness on the part of the player. But with what want of thoroughness, with what unthinking routine both pupils and teachers proceed through them! Either the instruction consists, all told, in more or less pedantically "ploughing through" the first book, and perhaps the second also, which naturally is then. as a rule, more quickly finished; or else the whole number, eighty-four, are really—in turn—hurriedly quitted; on accomplishing which, in nine cases out of ten, the but slight positive result appears, that the player who has reached No. 84, on being suddenly again confronted with No. 1, shows himself incapable of striking the first *arpeggioed* C major

* A copy of which, with manuscript revisions and additions, has been intrusted by the author to the present translator for the preparation of an English version.

triad in an artistically correct manner, not to mention other surprises for the examiner. Now, the practical ill-success so frequently attendant upon the study of Cramer's *Etudes* is owing to causes which it is the aim of this edition to obviate. First among these is the *non-observance of a systematic succession.* Such an one was not, at least consistently, carried out by the author. Moreover, in the English edition, the succession of the numbers differs from that in the German. The first-named edition, which lay before us in our work, and, indeed, as represented by a revisional copy provided with corrections in Cramer's own handwriting (this copy, belonging to Mr. Spitzweg, at that time at the head of the publishing house of Aibl, served as the standard for determining exactly all signs of time and expression), also .contains the sixteen studies supplementally issued in Vienna (surreptitiously in Hamburg), which have been comparatively but little disseminated, and the chief purpose of which, evidently, was only to make up the ceremonial number of 100. Accordingly, their non-consideration in the present edition was not prompted solely by their character of a private domain. For our attempt to remedy this evil, no claim is laid to *absolute* approval, since individual considerations will always play a certain rôle in instruction, if the teacher's conception of his task be not bureaucratic. A second chief cause of the qualitative resultlessness of the study of Cramer's *Etudes* is to be found in their over-great quantity. The same consideration in the case of Clementi's "Gradus ad Parnassum" has recently induced the Court-pianist to the King of Prussia, Mr. Carl Tausig, to edit an anthology of that work, accompanied with valuable directions for their correct practice, which is published in Berlin by Bahn (Trautwein's), and the adoption of which, on the part of all intelligent pianoforte-teachers, is to be recommended. With correct tact, Mr. Tausig has eliminated the intrinsically very valuable pieces in the severe contrapuntal style; for the pianoforte-fugues and canons of Clementi, far from offering a fit means of preparation for the Well-tempered Clavichord of Bach, are more likely to hinder the player by leading to bad habits. For "Bach-playing" demands preliminary studies which must be sought only in other compositions by that master himself—with, perhaps, the anticipation of pieces by Handel.* In preparing this edition of Cramer. all pieces for practice in which no perfectly definite mechanical end was pursued have been similarly culled and disposed of. Perhaps we may even

* As there was once, in Florence and at other Italian universities, a Dante faculty (Boccaccio was the first occupant of this chair of instruction), the members of which confined their philological labors simply to the enigma of this mighty sphinx, so there might be in place, in high schools of music, a similar specialization of the study of the German intellectual giant in tones, Bach, who is comparable to a Dante only. To play Bach beautifully and with finish is a task which—the necessary cerebral conditions abstracted—is only to be demanded from those pianists who have attained complete mastery over the material, and who also, for example, no longer brokenly stumble through Beethoven's last pianoforte-sonatas. Whither attempts to assimilate the works of Bach from the standpoint of the pianoforte-chair specifically tend, is most alarmingly shown by Czerny's celebrated edition of them, the transitory. merit of which we would not question, but against an uncritical use of which an emphatic warning must be given in the interest of a true understanding of Bach. Moreover, with the above remark, it is not intended to say that the introduction to the playing of Bach (preludes and inventions) may not, according to individual data, begin even simultaneously with the study of Cramer's *Etudes*.

be reproached for not having proceeded radically enough and for having given too much space to repeated representations of that which is homogeneous. To this it might be replied, that practical experience demonstrates the advantage of such readings. Precisely in connection with the necessity of acquiring by perseverance any special kind of mechanical expertness, the charm of a certain variety in homogeneity tends to refresh and stimulate, on the one hand, and on the other to promote and determine, and also, occasionally, as a counter-experiment, to instruct. After several homogeneous exercises only, the player should always revert, in recapitulation, to the first of them. Respecting a few other studies, of which the mechanical end is perhaps still more systematically developed in Clementi's Gradus—coupled, to be sure, with greater difficulties—it may be remarked, that in a regularly graded succession of those collections of studies which are to be employed for complete cultivation in pianoforte-playing, J. B. Cramer is the forerunner of Clementi. In this connection, perhaps, it may not be unwelcome to pianoforte-teachers to see indicated the course of mechanical study which the undersigned has found approved in his practice as a teacher. The course in question comprises all the studies, from those of the beginner to those of the *virtuoso*.

After the first rudiments have been mastered, for which purpose the first part of the pianoforte-method of LEBERT-STARK is most to be recommended as, to the best of our knowledge, the most substantial help, the following are in place:

I. *a*. The studies of ALOYS SCHMITT, Op. 16, together with the "Exercices Préparatoires",—always to be practised in all twelve keys—which form the introduction to the first book. It is worthy of mention that FELIX MENDELSSOHN-BARTHOLDY, who was an eminent master as pianist also, laid with this work the foundation of his classical technique.

b. In contrast to the relative dryness of Schmitt ▪ collateral use of STEPHEN HELLER, Op. 45.

II. *a*. J. B. CRAMER's studies.

b. ST. HELLER: Op. 46 and 47.

c. C. CZERNY: Daily Exercises; likewise his collection of studies, entitled the "Method of Legato and Staccato" (Die Schule des Legato und Staccato), which, strangely enough, has not hitherto received that notice which it merits.

III. *a*. CLEMENTI; "Gradus ad Parnassum" (selection and elaboration by C. Tausig).

b. MOSCHELES: Op. 70, 24 studies; a work more widely disseminated in North than in South Germany, which unconditionally deserves the predicate "classic".

IV. *a*. HENSELT: Selected studies from Op. 2 and 5.

b. Together with, and as preparatory to these, HABER-BIER: "Études-Poésies"; a kind of continuation of St. Heller.

c. Selected pieces by MOSCHELES: Characteristic studies (Charakteristische Studien). Op. 95.

V. CHOPIN: Op. 10 and 25, with which may be associated the study of the single Preludes (of a special mechanical tendency) from his Op. 28.

VI. LISZT: Six Etudes after Paganini; three Concert-Etudes; twelve grand Etudes, "d'exécution transcendante."

VII. *a*. RUBINSTEIN: Selected Etudes and preludes.

b. V. C. ALKAN: Selections from his twelve grand Etudes; for the most part more difficult than any of the aforenamed.

Simultaneously with entering upon stage III., THEODOR KULLAK's Method of Octaves (in three parts) should be attacked and prosecuted without haste, but also without interruption. This extremely meritorious special work is, in our opinion, irreplaceable, and it most justly claims the frequently misused title, "indispensable du pianiste". To refer here to other specialties of a subordinate nature, for purely mechanical ends, would extend this preface too far.

Finally, a third circumstance might be mentioned in justification of our instructive edition, and, indeed, the one which seems to us weightiest of all. It relates to the directions for the application of the fingers, which, being doled out by the author with a sparingness only proportionate to their want of consistency, were in need alike of augmentation and alteration, in order to help the performer to attain the purposed mechanical aim. In order to prevent misinterpretation, we will elucidate more particularly this apparently irreverent reproach against J. B. Cramer. His labors fell on the boundary-line between the earlier and later periods of pianoforte-playing, of which the latter, keeping pace with the increasing perfection of the instrument, and the enhanced demands resulting from it upon the performer's powers of execution, has, in course of time, arrived at a system of fingering in many respects diametrically opposed to the former. As the chief mechanical difficulty in piano-forte-playing, we now lay stress upon the unevenness, resulting from the local relations of black and white keys, of the field forming the scene of action for the performer's fingers. Our aim, therefore, is chiefly directed to rendering the fingers independent of that unevenness, and, by means of protracted gymnastic exercise, to enable them to move about on the black keys in a manner as light, free, secure, and distinct as when on white keys, and without stumbling in any combination whatsoever of white and black. According to the perhaps somewhat venturesome opinion of the editor, that is the best fingering which permits the performer, without mechanical preparation, and without previously taking pains to deliberate, to transpose a given pianoforte-piece to any key he may choose; a modern virtuoso of the genuine calibre must be able to perform Beethoven's Op. 57, for example, as conveniently in F♯ minor as in F minor. In such a case, the construction of a suitable fingering, which must be based exclusively upon a correct rendering of the musical phrase—without respect either to the relations of black and white keys, or to those of longer and shorter fingers—demands, of course, the overthrow of all the rules of the old method. This old method appears, after all, to have set out with the chief purpose of circumventing all difficulties endangering the preservation of a quiet position of the hand, through varying relations of the white and black keys which come into play; just as, among other things, it ignored the necessity of different applications of the fingers in the case of different modes of touch (*i. e.*, between *legato, staccato*, etc.); and just as it rejected that right of the thumb to "free migration", which is indispensable in polyphonic playing and for avoiding perplexities in transposition; declaring, as a matter of course, him to be the best pianoforte-composer whose inspiration was continually guided by the external image of the twelve half-steps of the the octave on the key-board, as seven broad and flat keys, together with five narrow and elevated ones; judged by which criterion, Clementi's pianoforte-fugues might indeed have claimed an unconditional superiority over those of a J. S. Bach.

Now, J. B. Cramer (born 1771, in Mannheim; died 1858, near London) comprehended in a far greater degree than did his predecessor, representing a more important artistic individuality, Muzio Clementi (born 1752, at Rome; died 1832, in England)—whose instruction, moreover, he enjoyed only in 1783-4, at Vienna, therefore as a boy—the necessity of breaking with that method; and in his studies are to be found frequent traces of reformatory directions for the fingering—especially, too, in respect to the old limitation of the activity of the thumb, just menfioned. But as if, frightened by the boldness of his attacks, he feared the result of consistently carrying them out, and finally yielded to the tyranny of earlier practical usage, he forthwith and frequently shows relapses into the old ways. Now, in preparing this edition, the editor deemed himself obliged to suppress the author who looked back, in favor of the one showing intuitions of the future; still, he has never gone so far as to force another fingering upon those pieces in which the invention of the pianoforte figures appears essentially induced by the practices of the old method; just as, according to his principles, the Hummel concertos (not, on the other hand, those of Mozart—we mean in the original, not their antiquating "Hummel"-ization [Ver-"hummel"-ung]) should be played with Hummel's own fingering—as sufficiently set forth in his method for the pianoforte—without any modernizing facilitation or aggravation whatsoever.

The instructive remarks appended to each study spare us the trouble of generalizing that in our work which, in its special place, in connection with practical use, will become self-evident. Still, we desire to mention, in passing, that, in point of the dynamic signs of delivery, we have thought it best to carry out with more exactness, and in detail, the intentions rather sketchily made known by the author. Similar revision seemed to us necessary in respect to the *legato*-slurs and *staccato*-points. Special care has been taken to display the text in a form as immediately intelligible as possible, following in this the modern principle of writing upon the upper staff all notes assigned to the right hand for performance, and all given to the left hand upon the lower staff; further, in parallel movements of two parts, of dispensing with the luxury of double "slurring"; etc.

With reference to the metronomic signs, which, as has been said already, are copied exactly from the original, we can not conceal that to us they appear excessively fast in the majority of cases—not merely in respect to the time to be taken in practising them, but also to that appropriate to their delivery simply as pieces of music. It is possible that, as happened with Beethoven, and more recently with Schumann (who is said to have metronomized after a defective Maelzel during an entire creative period), the relation of the compass of J. B. Cramer to our normal pyramid may have resembled that of a Fahrenheit to a Réaumur.

Concerning the life and labors of the composer, information is to be found in FÉTIS: Universal Biography (Biographie Universelle), first edition, 1866 [2nd ed., 1889]; Gassner's Universal Encyclopedia of Music (Universal-Lexikon der Tonkunst), etc. The History of Pianoforte-playing (Geschichte des Klavierspiels), by C. F. Weitzmann, was referred to at the outset; we fully subscribe to what is there said on the relation of Cramer to his predecessors and successors.

Unfortunately, we have not been able, despite repeated endeavors, to ascertain with exactness any thing concerning the dates of the successive publication of Cramer's studies, to establish which would be of more than mere historic interest. The second book appeared with Breitkopf and Härtel in 1810 (when in England?); and in the advertisement referring to it in the General Musical Gazette (Allgem. musikal. Zeitung), the first book is mentioned as having already passed through five editions, and as being one of the most excellent collections of studies that had appeared in the last "quinquennium" (1805–1810).

HANS VON BÜLOW.

MUNICH, May, 1868.

Fifty Selected Pianoforte-Studies

by

J. B. Cramer.

(1.) Each hand should first practise its part alone, in slow tempo and with a uniform degree of loudness. Then, by way of a test, try to play in faster tempo and an even *mezzo-piano* instead of the previous *forte.* If the slightest indistinctness should be detected, resume the first method of practice. Both hands must not play together until the mechanical difficulties are overcome. The study of execution with *crescendos* and *diminuendos,* etc., must then be worked out along the same lines; i. e., before the hands play together, each must have learned to perform its part alone with strict observance of the dynamic marks of expression. These rules apply, of course, to the study of all these Études.

(2.) The teacher must insist upon a *systematic* arpeggiation, wherever this figure occurs; and discourage with equal strictness, the habit of breaking the chords where no arpeggio is explicitly marked. The slightest latitude allowed in this matter, at the beginning of instruction, will work irreparable injury.

Execute the first arpeggio'd chord as follows: 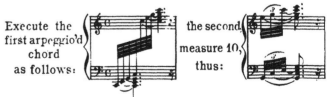 the second, measure 10, thus:

The difference in the execution of these two arpeggio'd chords depends, in part, on their different time-value, and in part on the different manner in which the chord-tones combine. The necessity for the *successive* arpeggio in measure 1, is evident from the lack of fullness which would result from a mode of execution similar to that in measure 10; because, in the former case, the right-hand part would merely double the left-hand part at an interval of 3 octaves.

1. To derive benefit from practising this number, it is of prime importance to firmly set and retain the outer fingers on their keys.

2. The movement of the middle fingers in both hands, while even and light, must always bring out the natural melodic expression of the figure: i. e., a slight *crescendo* in ascending, and a slight *diminuendo* in descending.

6

Moderato espressivo. (♪ = 138.)

1761

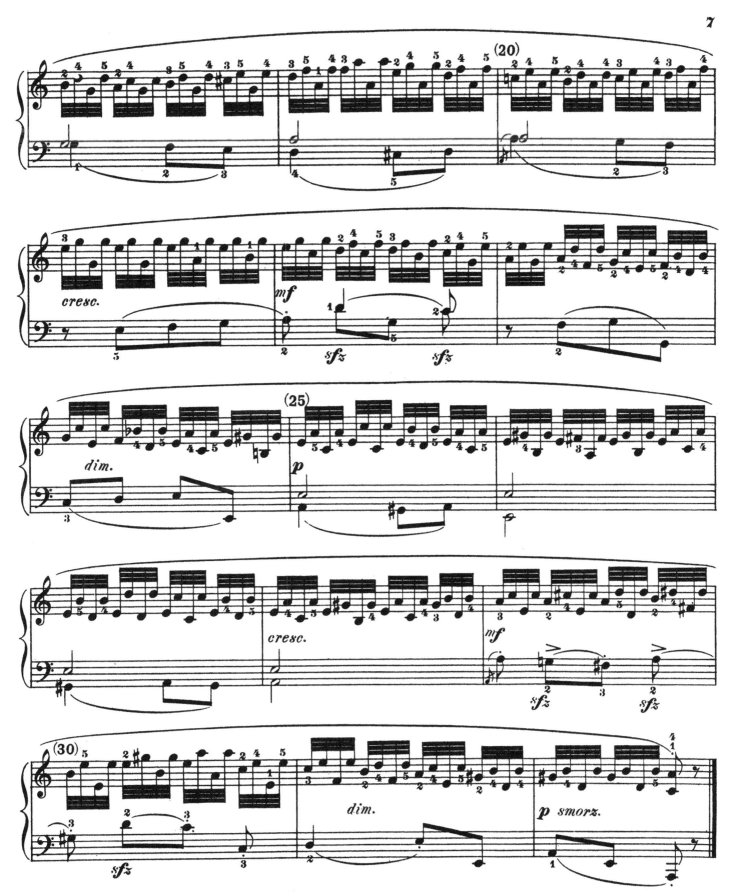

1. The apparent unimportance of the part assigned to the left hand in this Étude, should not mislead the pupil into imagining that the rule for the separate practice of each hand, given under Nº 1, may possibly be dispensed with here. On the contrary, its observance in this very case will tend to stimulate musical interest in the number, and thus indirectly further the execution of the right hand.

2. A partial alteration of the Cramer fingering — which at first glance may seem convenient — struck the editor as necessary here (as in various other cases,) in order to give the neglected fourth finger every possible opportunity for individual development. This emancipation of the fourth finger is an essential condition for a correct manner of holding the hand.

Allegro con spirito. ($\bullet$ = 132.)

4.
(13.)

f *e sempre legato*

(1.) A more practical distribution of the figures between the hands, in measures 14–17 and 25, appeared necessary both for rhythmical and purely mechanical reasons. Among the latter is the rule for avoiding the use of the thumb when crossing the hands; for this draws the entire palm of the hand into play, and thus impedes the ease of movement in both hands.

(2.) The fingering given for measures 10 and 11, is applicable to all similar graded progressions; the more black keys involved, the less will the thumb be used, and *vice versa*.

Allegro moderato. (♩ = 114)

5.
(22.)

pp

ten.

sempre legato

cresc.

(5)

f

(10)

pp

cresc.

f

(15)

ff

pp

A transposition of this Étude into G minor and F minor, would give a still better test of its practical utility; besides, practice in transposing cannot be too early recommended

as an advantageous influence on the pupil's ear and general musical development. Compare the Preface.

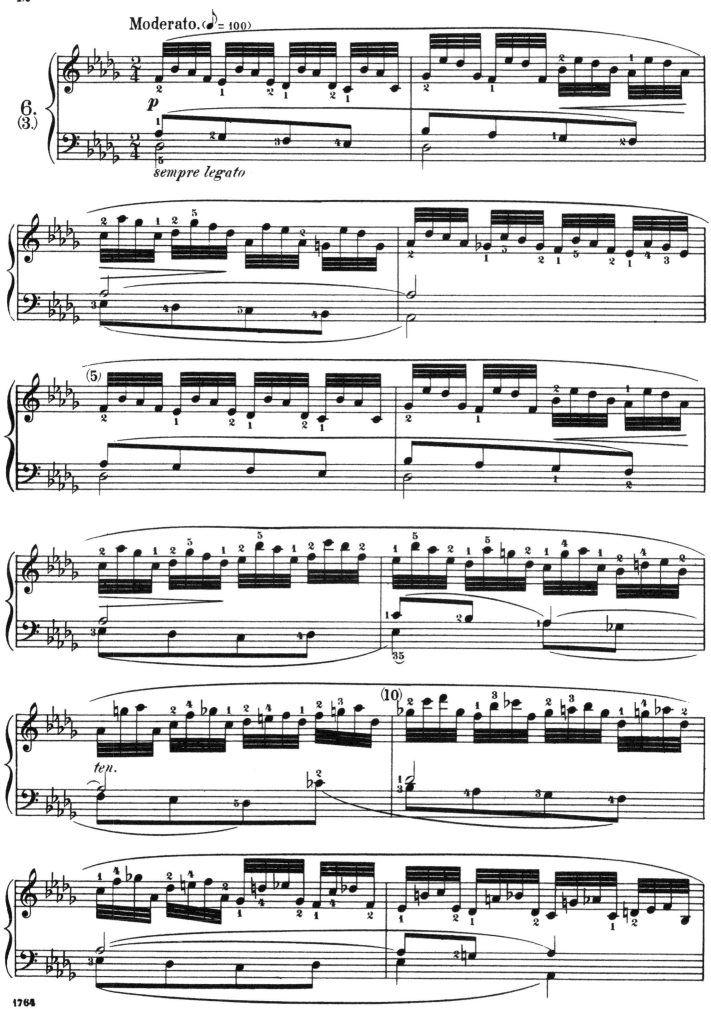

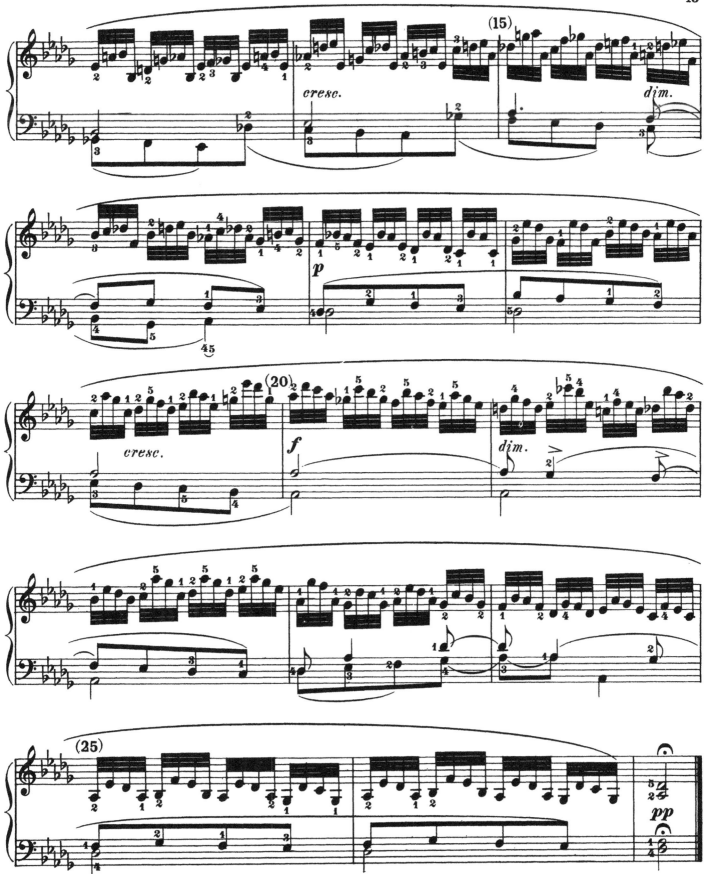

(1) The editor's experience in teaching has convinced him both of the comparative uselessness of this Étude in the original key of D major, and of its utility as transposed into D♭. In the original key, a good piano-fingering for small hands, in uninterrupted legato, could not be found for the transition between the very first two measures.

(2) Too great care cannot be bestowed on firmly holding down the thumb of the left hand in measures 9, 13 and 14, while the forefinger is turning over to take the last eighth-note. Sufficient attention is usually not paid to such "preliminary practice" to polyphonic playing.

(3) A transposition of this Étude into C major is also recommended. The unavoidable changes in the fingering may be left to the teacher's insight.

Moderato con espressione. (♩=132.)

7.
(16.)

(1.) This Étude is to be considered, first of all, as a study in velocity for the left hand. The teacher should take care, at the same time, to stimulate a feeling for the leading of the bass amid the endeavors after a smooth and even touch. This feeling should be expressed by an accentuation (though not too pointed) of tones marking successive modulations. Of course, such accents must not be unnecessarily multiplied; in measures 1 and 2, for instance, a repeated accent on this lowest note is not allowable. In measure 5, on the other hand, besides the first and third beats, the G and the A♮ (on the second and fourth half-beats respectively) are to be slightly marked, and in measures 6 and 7 each beat; whereas, in meas. 23 and 31, the second beat, on account of the unchanging harmony, admits of no accent.

(2.) Separate practice by the right hand will prove no less beneficial for an intelligent and elegant execution. The apparently complicated fingering must be strictly observed; it was derived from a consideration of the various modes of touch, and of the correct "declamation" of the melodic phrase.

(3.) The turn in meas. 29 may be played in two ways; either: or: ; the editor, however, prefers the latter, because it more strictly maintains the rhythmical integrity of the melodic succession (syncopation of the second beat); neither can the dissonance of A♭ against the bass G (second half of second beat) be considered offensive.

(1.) Touching the execution of the arpeggio'd chords in the first and last measures, compare the Note to Nº 1.

(2.) The *staccati* alternating between the hands, must be executed with the greatest precision (meas. 13-16.)

(3.) The Episode (meas. 21-25) deserves special at-tention, both on account of the change of fingering in the right-hand figure, and the leaps of the forefinger of the left hand in turning over.

(4.) Despite strong family resemblance to Etude 1, this number is not rendered superfluous by the latter.

18

Moderato. (♩ = 62)

9.
(28.)

(1.) To derive full profit from the exercises for the independence of the fourth and fifth fingers, we recommend that the number of movements in each measure should at least be doubled, thus: etc.

(2.) Hands of small stretching capacity will find only measures 1, 4, 12 and 28 of special difficulty. Admissible facilitations are left to the teacher's judgment in individual cases.

(3.) While pursuing the technical aims of this Étude, do not neglect the study of its classic form and its melodic and modulatory content.

(4.) Transpositions of this Étude into C♯ minor and B minor will prove very beneficial, both technically and as exercises in the practical utilization of elementary acquirements in harmony.

1. A certain continuity being both practical and necessary in every special study, the editor has placed the present and the next-following trill-exercise directly after the foregoing exercise for the fourth and fifth fingers. It will be seen at once, that a new feature of technical development appears in the present Étude: — the weaker fingers are combined with the stronger in a uniformly light and agile touch. Moreover, the fingers must be trained to contract swiftly after sudden extension; while the hand is to be so habituated to quiet plasticity of motion, that the finger-movements apparently leave it quite at rest.

2. The editor lays particular stress on an exact fingering for the left hand. His experience with the power of the law of inertia has taught him, that a fingering like the

usual convenient one: far too often leads to the following audible (or rather inaudible) result: By such an amateurish execution, in polyphonic pieces, are caused the most absurd misconceptions with regard to the leading of the parts. Passages in thirds — as, for example, those in the Presto of the Beethoven C♯ minor sonata op. 27, N? 2, mea's. 47, 48, 53 and 54, which have to be played *piano*, besides — require similar fingerings for their correct execution: more especially, because the deeper key-fall of our modern pianos renders it far more difficult to contend against the aforesaid law of inertia, than was probably the case when the Vienna pianoforte-action was generally employed.

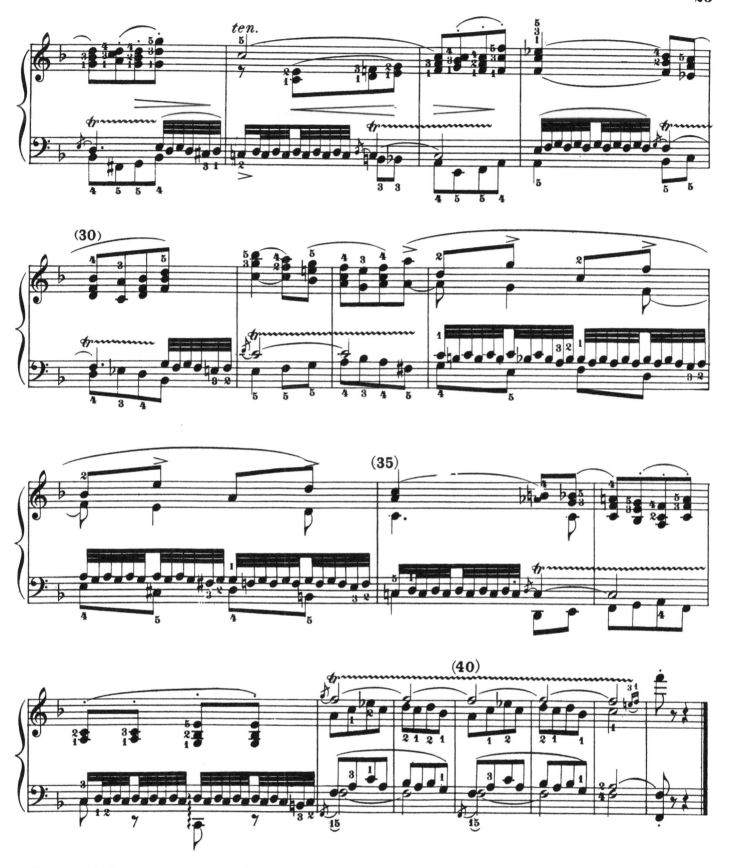

(1.) Instead of four trill-notes to each eighth-note, as in the original, the editor deemed it better to require six.

(2.) The beginning of the trill on the higher auxiliary, is justified by the importance of the trills in this number; by a proper regard for the smoothness of the after-beat; and by the suspension-like charm gained thereby; while no harmonic indistinctness is anywhere induced.

(3.) Exceptions are found in measures 25, 27, 35 and 37, in the left hand, where a beginning on the auxiliary would obscure the harmony in its most essential element— the bass.

(4.) In measures 13-15 a critical revision of the left-hand part appeared indispensable, it being of incomprehensible meagreness in the original.

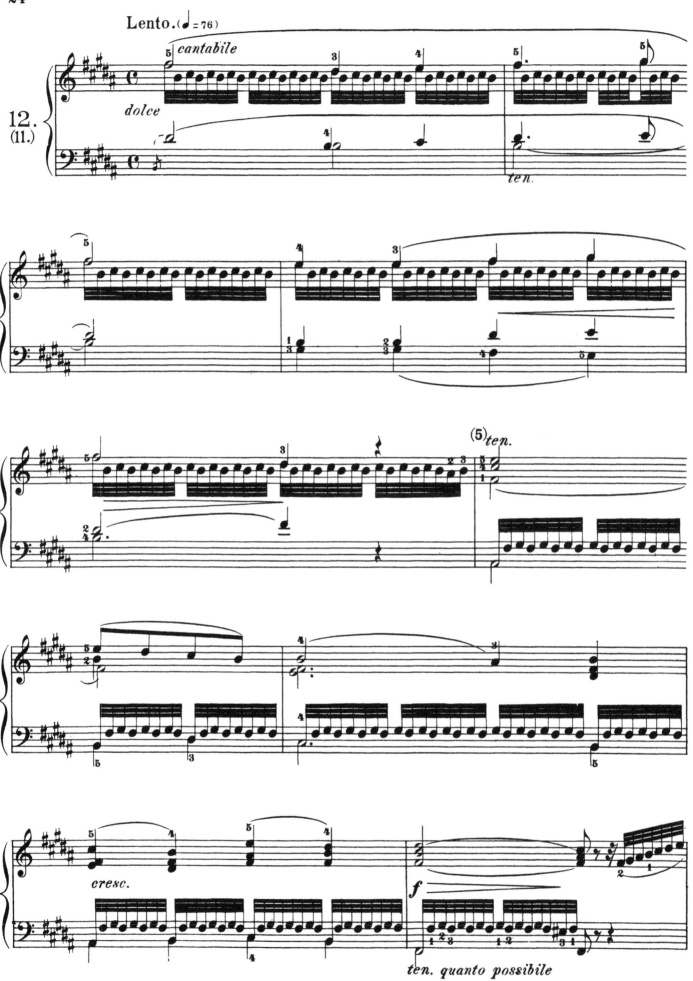

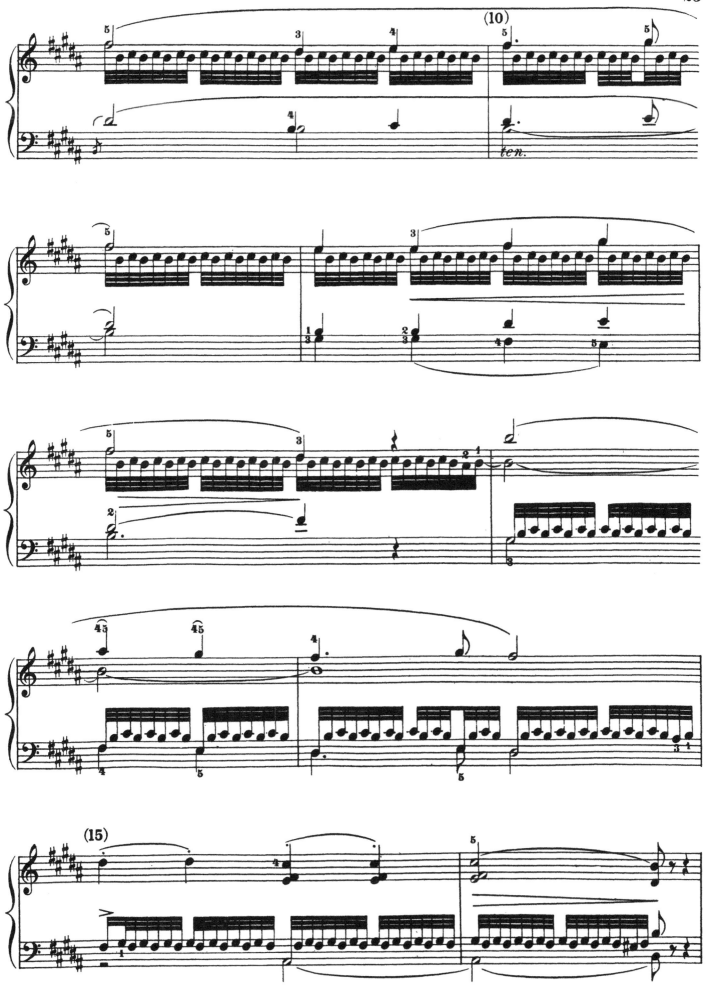

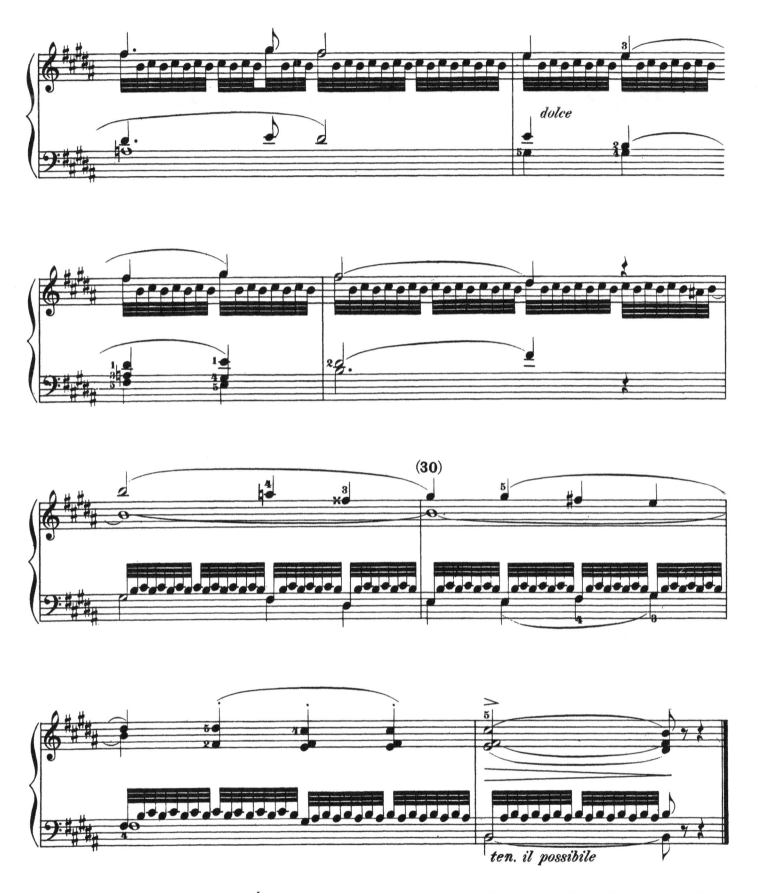

ten. il possibile

As a contrast to the preceding Étude, the present one seemed to be appropriate in this place. All so-called "strength," in piano-playing, depending on finger-agility obtained by practice, the independence of the fourth and fifth fingers, gained by means of the foregoing Études, will now be available in the shape of cleanness of attack, in playing the highest part. By writing out the trills in full, the editor hopes to remedy that pitiable indecision which frequently leads — in the final movements of the Beethoven sonatas op. 53, 109, 111, and also in the first movement of op. 106, for example — to the most sadly perverted practical interpretations.

28

Vivace. (♪.=100.)

13.
(33.)

mf
ten.

sempre sopra la mano destra

(5)

(10)

1764×

(1.) This uncommon $\frac{9}{16}$ time is to be treated quite similar-ly to the more frequent $\frac{9}{8}$ time. Besides the principal ac-cents on the 1st, 4th and 7th 16th-notes, slight secondary accents are required on the 3rd, 6th and 9th 16th-notes.

(2.) It would also be technically advantageous — as a secondary exercise in the smooth alternation of the hands, so that the passages may sound as if performed by one hand — to imagine the number written in $\frac{3}{8}$ or $\frac{6}{16}$ time, instead of $\frac{9}{16}$, and, instead of the prescribed accentuation;

 to accent as follows:

(1.) The modern school of execution generally accepts without qualification A. B. Marx's dictum, that technical and intellectual study should never be separated, but rather go hand in hand, so as to avoid the danger of being stupefied and blunted by exclusive application to the mechanical side of music; hence, an appropriate and correct technical performance of this Étude should likewise reproduce the characteristic, which it so plastically represents, of waves stormily rising and falling.

(2.) The accompaniment in the left hand is to be practised alone, and with the conscientiousness repeatedly and urgently recommended even for apparently unessential passages.

(3.) Concerning the appoggiaturas in measures 1, 3, 11, 13, etc., we may remark, that even the shortest — like all other ornaments, to which class they belong — must be struck on the beat of, and take its time-value from, the next-following principal note, and must not come in at the end of the preceding measure. The momentary dissonance:

need give no concern; but the octave-progression would be bad.

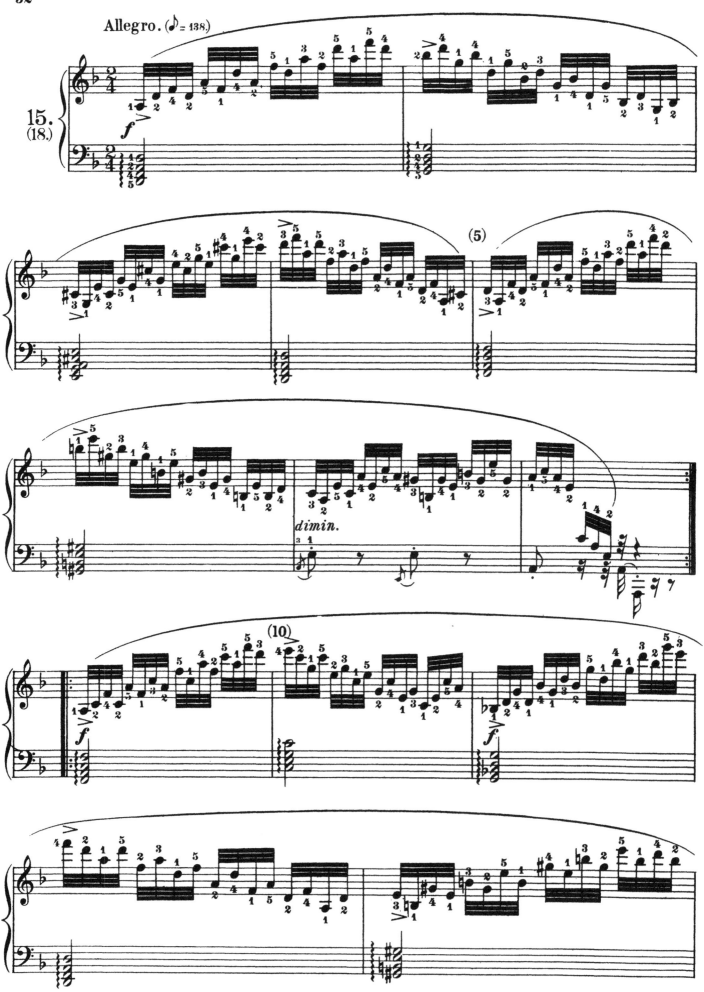

1. In this Étude and the next one, the rule given under № 1 for the correct execution of arpeggios will find most convincing justification, should it require any. The slovenly harmonic effects which necessarily arise from a premature striking of the lower chord-tones together with notes in the figured part belonging to another chord, must offend any delicate ear, and will move the teacher never to show the slightest toleration for such carelessness on the pupil's part.

The correct execution is again shown:

Measure 1.

or even, in still slower tempo, like this:

Measure 3.

2. With beginners, special care must be taken to have this number practised in the very slowest tempo at first, with a most vigorous finger-stroke and infallible accuracy, also raising each finger quite high before striking each individual tone.

3. After overcoming the first mechanical difficulties, and familiarization with the changing intervals, etc., practise the ascending passages *crescendo,* and the descending ones *diminuendo.*

4. The rule given for arpeggios is also applicable to the short appoggiaturas in measure 7. See also Note 3 to № 14.

Allegro. (♩ = 138.)

16.
(56.)

All remarks on the preceding Étude apply to its counterpart, the present number. We also add the (wellnigh superfluous) recommendation, to let the pupil practise the measures two by two.

1764

(1) It will be well to repeat the first two notes of each figure twice, in the following manner:

(2) With regard to the fingering for the left hand in measures 4, 8, 16, 24, and 28, refer to Note 2 under Nº 10.

(3) The teacher should also insist that, for triads in close position, in the left hand, the pupil must not amateurishly use the fifth finger, but the fourth.

(4) In this number, as well as all the others, the left-hand part must be practised alone, for the sake of clear rhythmic "declamation." Time so spent will bring its reward.

Allegro moderato. (♩=132.)

18.
(9.)

(1.) As no short, typical figure predominates in this Étude, but, instead, a variety of successive figures, it appears advisable to make a special preliminary study of each of the small groups. For instance, practise measure 1 at first alone, and then in connection with measure 2; then take up the figure in measure 3, with amplifications; then the one occuring in measure 9; etc.,

(2.) It is evident, that the right-hand part also requires special practice; careful attention must, in particular, be paid to correct phrasing, (musical punctuation,) which is precisely indicated by beginning and ending of the legato-slurs.

(3.) The following execution of the trills in measures 2, 6, 8, etc., is perhaps more tasteful than that written out in measure 2:

Through the retarded entrance of the C♯, the auxiliary D receives added melodic importance as a suspension. This mode of execution is particularly recommended for measure 26, in order to avoid accidental consecutive fifths between bass and soprano: $\frac{d}{g}$ $\frac{c\sharp}{f\sharp}$.

This Étude, as № 2 (in the original,) was not in the right place. The change from swift extension to contraction of the hand, and the work expected of the weaker fingers, demand a higher degree of technical development than № 1 presupposes. But, after Nos. 9, 10, and 17 have gone before, the task can be accomplished without difficulty. We hardly need point out the necessity for practising the left-hand part by itself.

20.

(1.) The chromatic steps in the right–hand figure should be specially accented at first.

(2.) Do not underrate the secondary importance of this Étude as a staccato study for the left hand. The player should imagine the effect of a *pizzicato* on the violoncello. Pay careful attention to the fingering.

(1.) Double-notes like these are easier for beginners to master than passages in thirds, for instance; for in the former the strength of the entire hand can aid the weakness of individual fingers. Give particular attention to lifting the hand elastically after each connected group of two notes, executing the figures as follows:

etc. It is even advisable, by way of

practice, to allow a still longer pause to intervene; e.g.

(2.) The left hand has an opportunity to continue the staccato exercises begun in the preceding number. The occasional 32nd notes in measures 8, 10, etc., demand energetic rapidity.

1764

(1.) Finished execution of this beautiful piece demands, to be sure, quite maturely developed theoretical intelligence on the player's part; but this development can be successfully promoted by the mere technical practice of the Étude. It is the teacher's duty to give harmonic explanation suited to individual pupils; e. g., to point out the passages where the bass note is to be imagined as still sounding, to explain each change of tonality, and, above all, to stimulate a susceptibil-

ity for the melodic leadings of the separate parts, and for their contrapuntal combination.

(2.) The necessity for separate practice with each hand is self-evident.

(3.) In measures 15-17 the editor deemed it practical to eliminate the extremely awkward crossing of the hands — even at the risk of offending the eye — by a simple exchange in the part-leading.

(1) This Étude doubtless forms the best introduction to practising passages in thirds. By the staccato lift of each fourth 16th-note (which, by the way, makes an excellent exercise in elastic touch), fatigue is obviated. As a preliminary study, an amplification of the first half of the figure is recommended: As secondary studies, the following variants may be tried: and:

(2) The octave-progressions in the left hand are to be played as energetically and decidedly as possible. The teacher should prevent the formation of that well-meant, amateurish bad habit of trying to connect an octave with a higher one by replacing the thumb by another finger, and thus (unavoidably) quitting the lower note of the lower octave. (No less reprehensible is the reverse practice of replacing, in descending, the fifth finger of the left hand by the third, thus quitting the higher octave-note.)

24.
(63.)

Allegro vivace. (♩=160.)

(1.) In the rapid tempo prescribed, the pupil, in his presumable stage of technical proficiency, will hardly be able to master this Étude. Its practice in slower tempo need not, however, be considered premature. The teacher will do well, after the lapse of a certain time devoted to the further study of this collection of Études, to return to this number; and, in general, to review systematically.

(2.) Particular attention must be paid to lifting the finger in exact time, and both to feel and to see that it is so lifted, at the end of a legato-slur.

(3.) Regarding the left-hand arpeggios in the shape of appoggiaturas, we refer to the previous remarks (Notes to Nos. 1 and 14). As the short appoggiatura represents the bass of the chord, it should be marked all the more decidedly from the fact, that the after-striking tone is more impressed on the ear by its longer duration. — The triplets in the right hand are to be executed as follows:

Maestoso energico. (♩=108.)

25.
(64.)

(1.) The strong emphasis and staccato lift of the bass note (the first in each group of 16th-notes), must induce no delay in the entrance of the accompanying figure, which latter is to be regarded as an independent middle part.

(2.) When the figurate motive is taken up by the right hand, the first 16th-note must still be marked, but not played staccato except in meas. 9-12.

(3.) For the prevention of rhythmic misconceptions, $\frac{12}{8}$ time has been substituted, in the proper passages, for the original $\frac{4}{4}$ time.

(4.) To overcome the difficulty of the change from legato to staccato in the left hand (meas. 13-15), it is advisable *at first* to practise the following accentuation (triplet of quarter-notes):

Allegro con brio. (♩=152.)

26.
(54.)

The preparations for the technical mastery of this Étude are contained in Nos. 21 and 23. The Note under No. 1, on elasticity of touch, is again specially applicable to the passages in sixths in measures 17-19, and 33-35; with reference to the passages in thirds, we refer to No. 23. True, the left hand has had no opportunity, in the foregoing Études, for preliminary studies on the task here assigned to it; but for this purpose recourse may be had to Aloys Schmitt's "Exercices préparatoires," in Part I of his collection of Études, as it may be taken for granted, that every expert teacher uses them in elementary instruction. Special care must be taken to execute the triplet in 32nd-notes in clean and well-rounded style, wherever it occurs.

Allegro assai. (♩=152.)

27.
(65.)

1. The advice given by Louis Köhler in his "Anthology of Cramer's Études" ("Klassische Hochschule," Book I), to practise the first figure as if it were

written legatissimo: R.H. 🎵, L.H. 🎵

completely coincides with our views.

2. In connection with the above, we advise several repetitions — say four, whereby the whole measure

1764

would be doubled — of the figure on the second beat:

🎵 2 3 4 1 2 3 4 1

3. Also practise meas. 8 with the R.H. descending and the L.H. ascending; measures 9, 11, 33 and 34 should be utilized for special studies, repeating each group of quarter-notes once, so as to preserve the integrity of the rhythm; a point always to be borne in mind in all mechanical practice.

Moderato assai. ($\flat$=126.)

28.
(76.)

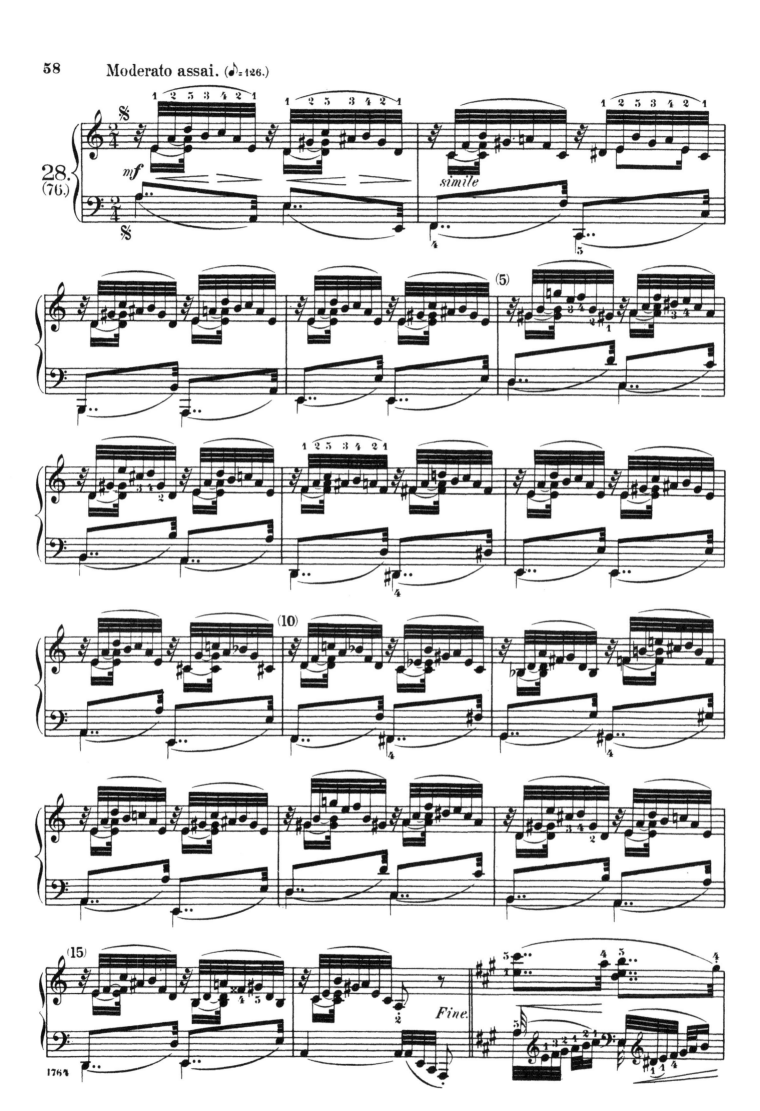

simile

(5)

(10)

(15)

Fine.

Considering only the first division of this Étude, one would classify it among the easier studies, although various stretches, as in meas. 5, demand well-developed fingers. The really noteworthy difficulties, however, are to be found in the middle division. The left hand will discover gymnastic exercises of a peculiar kind in the necessity for sliding the thumb, and in its progressions to black keys. Special attention must be devoted, in the middle division, to precision in the completion of the bass figure by the after-striking higher part; likewise to the somewhat similar reverse condition in the principal division.

Allegro con brio. (♩ = 152.)

29.
(23.)

(1.) Köhler's method, recommended under № 27, may also be profitably applied here.

(2.) As a preliminary exercise, take the following simplification of the figure:

(3.) To avoid an awkward lift and leap in the ascending connection of the figures, and to learn how to execute the

prescribed *legato*, a preliminary study in binding each fourth 32nd-note to the one following it, will prove effective:

(4.) It will be profitable, both from a technical and a musical point of view, to transpose this Étude into other keys.

Allegro con spirito. ($\flat$ = 160)

(1.) This Étude closely follows the preceding in its instructive aim, by further developing the flexibility of the fingers of the right hand. For the attainment of any species of technical proficiency one requires, above all, continuity in the practice of similar passages, but at the same time a certain variety, so as not to dull the player's interest. Such variety is presented here by the necessity of accenting with the third and fourth fingers, for which purpose they must, of course, be decidedly raised before striking.

(2.) The trills in measures 11 and 12 must begin on the principal note, because fundamental bass tones must not be obscured.

(3.) For the execution of the short appoggiaturas in the last measures, compare the Notes under Nos. 14 and 24.

1. This uniquely important study on the development of fluency in the left hand, may be most profitably practised, at first, with the omission of the low bass note (fifth finger;) still, at the beginning of every measure, see to it that the hand is extended to about the width of an octave. (A similar procedure should be adopted for the right hand in Moscheles' op. 70, N⁰. 3, and Chopin's op. 10, N⁰. 2.) The task of the fourth finger requires special attention. When playing in the prescribed tempo (refer to the Preface touching this point,) the short bass note can occupy only the time-value of a 32nd-note, on account of the *staccato* and the necessity for swift contraction of the hand. But take care not to arpeggiate these octaves by playing the lower tone like an appoggiatura.

2. We need not explain, that the right-hand part requires very special study. Regarding the fingering, see Note 2 under N⁰ 10. Despite the slur, a note repeated in one and the same part, as in measures 9-11, etc., must always be re-struck, as may be inferred from the fingering given.

3. Musically advanced players will find it no waste of time to transpose this Étude into C minor and E minor.

Allegro con fuoco. (♩ = 108.)

32.
(49.)

1. In order to turn to best account the rich instructive material contained in this Étude, each individual figure should be amplified into a special exercise, and extended over the keyboard as far as practicable. For instance, measure 1 may be begun an octave higher and carried down an octave lower, and meas. 4 likewise; meas. 7, (and also meas. 19 and 21,) may be repeated by itself a dozen times. The left-hand passages in measures 11-13 and 27-29, should also be practised in other keys, in which tonic and dominant are on a white key.

2. Chords not provided with the arpeggio-sign should be struck flat and very decidedly, almost drily.

3. The major sixth found in descending in the third beat of measures 1 and 5, though unpleasing to some ears, is so explicitly required by the author, that it appears unjustifiable to alter it to a minor sixth. The player must simply get used to it, as it is not a "false" interval.

1764

70

1764

(1.) Although the chief aim of this Étude is to train the hands to smooth and even execution when playing together or alternating with and rhythmically supplementing each other, in which respect it is to be regarded as a counterpart to No. 13, this aim can be attained only after previous pratice by *each hand separately* until it can play its part with absolute correctness.

(2.) In arranging this number in accordance with the modern style of notation introduced for piano-music by Liszt and Raff, in order to attain a better sound-effect and a more plastic view of the interweaving of the higher and lower parts, the editor adopted a suggestion by Köhler in his "Klassische Hochschule", Book I.

(3.) Hands of small stretching capacity may practise binding tenths in the following manner: as a side-study.

1. While related to the preceding Étude as regards the interweaving of the parts, this number also affords new material for practice:

(a) In that light staccato touch which should resemble the portamento;

(b) For the right hand, in changing fingers on one and the same key.

2. By indicating in detail and consistently, by the terms *sotto* and *sopra*, whether the left hand has to play below or above the right, we trust to have obviated the embarrassment of the player which usually deters him from practising this number.

3. At the beginning, slow practice with a vigorous touch is recommended.

4. Hands of lesser stretching capacity should use the descending ninths and tenths, in measures 3, 4, 46 and 17, as independent finger-exercises, in the manner explained for the left hand in the preceding Étude.

Allegro molto agitato. (♩ = 108.)

35.
(55.)

1. One of the best means for acquiring lightness of touch, is to practise changing fingers on the same key. From this point of view, the present Étude stands in instructive connection with the preceding.

In order to acquire a proper staccato of the first note in the triplet, and to avoid the more convenient slurring to the second note, the following variant is recommended as a preparatory exercise:

2. With regard to the fingering of the accompaniment (which latter, as usual, demands special study), the edit-

or permits modifications, providing that they be systematically carried out.

3. The chords in the right hand (meas. 43-50) must be played, notwithstanding their staccato execution, with the given fingering, if the player would attain infallible accuracy in such passages. In fact, the teacher should always make a point of opposing the pupil's tendency to naturalism, even in matters apparently unessential. That semi-unconscious dexterity of finger which seems to be the birthright of great pianistic talents, must likewise be *systematically trained*, if anything more than "cultivated dilettanteism" is aimed at.

Allegro strepitoso. (♩ = 144.)

36.
(69.)

(1.) In its technical aims the present Étude belongs, like the two next-following, to the class already represented in Nos. 23 and 26 (also Nos. 21 and 24). The teacher should let the pupil review the earlier numbers, with the Notes appertaining thereto.

(2.) The trills for the right hand in measures 17 to 19 should occupy, in rapid tempo, only the time-value of a simple turn; but the resulting quintuplet must be strictly rhythmically apportioned to the lower part, and both forms of quintuplet (2+3 and 3+2) ought to be practised. Of

course, more notes are to be played in slow tempo.

(3.) The melodic ornament in the first beat of meas. 26 and 28, and in the third and fourth of meas. 31 and 32, is technically termed à "slide" (in German: "Schleifer"; see C. Ph. E. Bach's indispensable text-book: "Versuch über die wahre Art, das Clavier zu spielen"). As a rule (and here, too) it is to be executed crescendo.

(4.) For the appoggiaturas in the bass, meas. 29-30, see Note 3 to № 24.

(30)

(35)

(1.) In the main, follow the Notes to the preceding Étude. The teacher should in no wise tolerate the tendency of unskilful fingers to arpeggiate the passages in sixths.

(2.) The eighth-note marked staccato, in meas. 1, 2 and 8, is simply to be played as a sixteenth-note. A special effort to raise the finger concerned is reprehensible, if only in consideration of the legato in the lower part.

(3.) The editor's pedagogical experience leads him to lay special stress on a rule for slurred notes which cannot be misconstrued. *A slur over two notes affects only the relation of these two tones to each other,* and not that of the second to any third note following. The final note under a slur is, therefore, to be treated as short, thus assuming a staccato-mark, the actual writing-out of which would savor too much of pedantic excursiveness.

Allegro moderato, ma energico. (♩= 138)

(1.) Practise this Étude at first in the strongest *fortissimo*. It is the most difficult of its class in the entire collection. Special study must be devoted to the fourths in meas. 11-14. and elsewhere, during the separate practice of which the teacher might play the sixths below, so as to spare the pupil's ear the unpleasant sound-effects; — in fact, even in purely mechanical exercises, euphony ought never to be lost sight of. The so-called "dumb pianos", whose employment the editor warmly advocates, are, to be sure, the best resource in such cases.

(2.) As a piece of music, this Étude was assuredly inspired by the second Prelude in Bach's "Well-tempered Clavichord". This would seem a favorable opportunity to make the pupil acquainted with the latter composition.

(1.) As a kind of preparation for the work now in hand, measures 11 - 14, and 29 - 32, of the preceding Étude in the left-hand part, may be utilized.

(2.) The sustained higher tones in the right hand, and lower tones in the left, are to be struck very energetically, as the musical (i. e., acoustic) value of notes on the piano depends more on the first stroke (and its preparation by raising the wrist) than on holding down the key by the finger.

(3.) A most exact observance of the slurs, and of the fingering connected with them, is recommended. Separate practice is required by the half-measure (syncopated) in meas. 7-9 and elsewhere. Hands of more than normal stretching capacity may take, in this passage, the fingering 1 2 3 1 instead of 1 1 2 1.

(4.) In the original the sustained tones are not always repeated with that exactitude which doubtless conforms to the Author's intention, and which it appeared necessary to observe in this new edition.

(1.) The study of this number should be divided into two portions. Let each hand first practise the simpler portion of its part, i. e., meas. 1_9, 25_34 (to 37 for the left hand); and thereafter the passages where doubled notes occur, at first, however, practising only the running part. The tones of the added part are always to be sustained where no staccato is explicitly marked. For executing this latter, compare Note 2 to Étude 37.

(2.) The different length of the slurs in the two hands is based on easily intelligible technical reasons, and must not be overlooked when both hands play together.

(3.) When beginning practice, sharp accentuation of the strong beats, and even of the half-beats, is strongly to be recommended as an aid to the precision of touch. As the difficulties are gradually overcome, these accents may be lessened; for a technically finished execution they should be reduced to the minimum sanctioned by good taste.

1. The more difficult fingering substituted by the editor for the far simpler and easier one: is advantageous in promoting the contraction of the hand and thus increasing precision in touch; it has a leaning toward virtuosity, and was taken over from the editor's private practice (e. g., in the B major passage in the first movement of Beethoven's fourth piano-concerto, op. 58.) It gives greater brilliancy to the execution and more elastic lightness to the touch; though this does not nullify its value as an exercise with the *easier* fingering.

2. For executing the staccato accompaniment in the left hand, see Note 2 to № 20.

(1) The profit to be derived from this extremely useful Étude, will consist in an equally delicate and even distinctness of touch of the individual fingers with the greatest possible lightness of the wrist. As an exercise in repeated tones, it should be practised in connection with Nos. 35 and 36, which are now to be reviewed as appropriate preliminary studies. The binding of certain half-tone and whole-tone steps, (e. g., in meas. 23, and 17 and 19, respectively,) by a special slur, was retained and consistently carried out according to the original. The musical reason for this is so evident, that explanation would be superfluous.

(2) We earnestly warn the teacher against toleration for the "naturalistic" fingering: by reason of the bad habits it engenders in a technical and musical sense. Repeated use of the thumb, after the octave in the bass, for playing the harmonic accompanying and accessory parts, is permissible only when the latter kind are a direct repetition of the former, as in meas. 90 and 91, though, for that matter, the other fingering is also applicable to these cases. In meas. 23 and 27, there is no preceding octave; consequently, the above rule does not apply to them.

Andante maestoso ed espressivo. (♩=160.)

43.
(77.)

(1.) This Étude is doubly valuable: as a study in flexibility for the left hand, and as a study in melodic expression for the right. It must, of course, be left to the teacher's judgment, whether or no the number is too far advanced in the latter respect, for the musical development of any individual pupil. A fine interpretation of the *cantilena* assumes that the pupil is already qualified to interpret Field's Nocturnes, or the melodic passages in Hummel's or Moscheles' piano-concertos, not to mention the classics *par excellence*. It is advisable, at all events, to practise the left-hand part to such a degree of finished execution, that the "involuntarily" even performance of the triplet-figure shall no longer embarrass the right hand in playing two or four notes against each triplet with rhythmical exactness. The tenths at the beginning of the measure must not, of course, be taken by leaps, but by skilfully sliding and drawing the hand upward (see the exercise written out in Note 3, N? **33,** which ought now to be practised in sharp keys.)

1764

(2.) The long appoggiaturas in the higher part are written out in modern notation. As frequently remarked, the short ones must take their time-value, however brief, from the next-following principal note.

(3.) The turn in measure 5 is to be played thus: In quicker tempo it is to be treated like a quintuplet (see Note 2, N? 36.)

(4.) Execute the run in measure 18 so that the rapidity of movement increases as it ascends, something like this: Several other modes of execution might be adopted, provided that a discordant clash with bass notes be avoided.

The player having already encountered *similar* material for practice in this collection (e.g., Etude № 33, useful as a preparatory study,) his attention may turn immediatly to the study of expression and style, this requiring considerable flexibility of wrist and and even of the elbow-joint. The double-hooked mel-

ody-notes of the higher part should be struck off, as it were, with a most vigorous attack. For practice in correctly striking the accented intervals, a side-stud-y of the same in legato is recommended:

On the other hand, it will also be beneficial to practise this number staccato throughout.

The instructive aim of this Étude, which is also of no mean value as a piece of music, hardly requires detailed explanation. The following points may be left to the teacher's intelligent supervision: Polyphonic playing in the right hand; expressive emphasis of the sustained melody in the highest part; subordination of the second accessory part; delicate fluency and distinct continuity in the figurate accompaniment;— hence, the correct apportionment of the dynamic shad-

ing of each individual part, and compact consonance of the chords, unmarred by the slightest arpeggio. No less care ought to be bestowed on correct phrasing, as indicated by the beginning and end of the slurs, and likewise on strict observance of the note-values of the two parts in the left hand, the higher of which represents, as it were, a violoncello-part and the lower a double-bass. Transposition into other keys, already so often recommended as a means for musical development, will be found decidedly profitable in this case (e. g., into A and B minor.)

1764

(1.) This Étude forms a counterpart to the preceding; and although the right hand has here only two parts, the execution is more difficult, so that No. 46 serves far better for a preparatory study to No. 45, than *vice versa*, more especially because the figurate accompaniment in the former requires a more expressive shading. The player should imagine the effect of a string-quartet.

(2.) As a piece of music this may, in a sense, be regarded as the prototype of Mendelssohn's "Songs without Words", and, despite its modest simplicity, with which, however, it unites perennial freshness and dignity of ornamentation and finish of form and piano-style, it is assuredly no less valuable than any of the above-named pieces by the aforesaid more modern master.

(3.) The player must carefully avoid a sentimental retarding of the tempo. Moreover, the middle division (*Minore*) will bear an imperceptible acceleration.

(4.) The notes written here and there on the lower staff (in meas. 3, 4–15, 16, etc.), to avoid using too many leger-lines, are to be executed by the right hand.

(1.) The (at first glance) somewhat strange-looking slurs over skips, are given in the original, and have, therefore, been retained. The author probably intended to indicate the connected execution of a four-measure period, rather than the avoidance of lifting the hands (e. g., in the case of tenths), which latter is impracticable for small hands, though it should be made as imperceptible as possible. It will be best, in any event, when practising at first, to study the accents belonging to the motive by dividing up the slur as follows:

When the fingers have become more familiar with the technical difficulty, more and more attention should be paid to the aforesaid "connected execution", and while still energetically marking the accents, any noticeable lifting of the hand should be smoothed over.

(2.) The prescribed alternation of the 4th and 5th fingers for the octaves in the right hand (meas. 22-28, 62-66), is no mere notion, and is, therefore, commended to pedantic observance.

(3.) The fingering given for the left hand has been explained in former Notes (see Notes 2 to No 42; and, for the passage in meas. 17-20, Note 3 to No 37).

(1.) In its essential object this Étude is a continuation of the one preceding. As it may now be assumed, that the player is accustomed to execute wide intervals in rapid time, not by leaping, but by gliding with a quiet hand, the method of lifting the hand proposed as a preparatory exercise to № 47, is not to be employed here.

(2.) The player is expressly warned against using any fingering, but the one given, for the turn in the first half beat. It is, in particular, a wholly reprehensible, amateurish trick to let the forefinger play alternately above and below the thumb; besides always having a lame effect, it causes needless fatigue and tends to stiffen the touch.

Consequently, never play so: but rather: 3121, 3121. and still better: 4321, 4321.

(3.) Strict observance of the prescribed *crescendo* and *decrescendo* in nearly every measure, will also afford technical facilitation. (See 1 to № 13.)

(4.) Concerning the execution of arpeggio chords, the needful remarks have often been made.

(1.) Experience shows that both this Étude and the next one are peculiar — in not being practised. True, the difficulties they offer exceed those encountered in Clementi's "Gradus ad Parnassum", to which Cramer's Études form the introduction. But it will prove both possible and profitable to practise them in slow tempo. As a preparation, the following preliminary and side-studies are recommended:

a) Transposition of the figure to white keys:

b) Inversion: 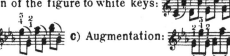 c) Augmentation:

(2.) For small hands, the tenths in the accompaniment may be changed, without detriment to the effect, into thirds, thus bringing the bass into the higher octave:

(measure 3-6):

As in the case of all arpeggio'd chords marked *"tenuto"*, the highest note should always be held; the bass note, a mere indication of which suffices for a cultivated ear, may be prolonged by an intelligent use of the pedal, (which is, to be sure, to be avoided in étude-playing). For the rest, see Note 3 to № 33, and Note 4 to № 34.

It is the teacher's duty to dispel, by means of theoretical and practical instructions and suggestions adapted to individual cases, the feeling of discouragement which generally overcomes the pupil at sight of this Étude. The player's interest will be most easily aroused, even for technical practice, by requiring him to explain every eighth-note according to the laws of harmony, i. e., by his previously figuring the bass. Furthermore, the task should be divided up into the smallest possible fragments (which, of course, must be musically complete); to this end, the phrasing-slurs will be helpful. Deviations from the given fingering are permissible only when another is regularly substituted; it is wholly inadmissible to make the execution dependent on the whim of the moment and blind luck in striking the keys.